Martinique History and Culture
The People origin and Custom

Author
Dominic Hussain

Copyright Notice

Copyright © 2017 Global Print Digital
All Rights Reserved

Digital Management Copyright Notice. This Title is not in public domain, it is copyrighted to the original author, and being published by **Global Print Digital**. No other means of reproducing this title is accepted, and none of its content is editable, neither right to commercialize it is accepted, except with the consent of the author or authorized distributor. You must purchase this Title from a vendor who's right is given to sell it, other sources of purchase are not accepted, and accountable for an action against. We are happy that you understood, and being guided by these terms as you proceed. Thank you

First Printing: 2017.

ISBN: 978-1-912483-49-5

Publisher: Global Print Digital.
Arlington Row, Bibury, Cirencester GL7 5ND
Gloucester
United Kingdom.
Website: www.homeworkoffer.com
.

Table of Content

Introduction 1

About Martinique 1

Land and Environment 4

Relief and drainage 5

Climate 7

Plant and animal life 8

People 10

Family, Marriage, and Kinship 11

Socialization, Etiquette, Religion and Socialization 13

Secular Celebrations 19

Arts and the Humanities 20

Social Stratification 24

Gender Roles and Statuses 25

Economy 27

Agriculture and fishing 27

Manufacturing 28

Tourism and trade 29

Transportation 30

Politics 35

Justice 40

Health and welfare 40

Education 40

Cultural Life 42

Carnival in Martinique *48*

Gommiers and yoles *53*

Rum of Martinique *57*

Nature of Martinique *61*

Tropical fruits *64*

History **70**

Early Period *70*

French rule *71*

Developments since World War II *74*

Alignment in more Detail *78*

Urbanism, Architecture, and the Use of Space *84*

Travel and Tourism **86**

Travel guide to Martinique *86*

Travel Tips *90*

Things you can do in Martinique *92*

Attractions *95*

Holidays and Festivals *101*

Food and Restaurants *104*

Shopping and Leisure *109*

Transportation *111*

Airports *114*

Getting around on Martinique *115*

Buying, Eating and Drinking *119*

Visas and Vaccinations *126*

Weather *128*

Facts about Martinique and tourism 134

The intricacy of human flows in the Martinique Island... 136

Sainte Luce: from a fishing village to a tourist resort 142

From the Martinique Island to the Caribbean Area 144

Ending the Fact 151

Introduction
About Martinique

|Martinique, is an island and overseas territorial collectivity of France, in the eastern Caribbean Sea. It is included in the Lesser Antilles island chain. Its nearest neighbours are the island republics of Dominica, 22 miles (35 km) to the northwest, and Saint Lucia, 16 miles (26 km) to the south. Guadeloupe, another part of overseas France, lies about 75 miles (120 km) to the north.

The name Martinique is probably a corruption of the Indian name Madiana ("Island of Flowers") or Madinina ("Fertile Island with Luxuriant Vegetation"), as reputedly told to Christopher Columbus by the Caribs in 1502. The administrative capital and chief town is Fort-de-France. Area 436 square miles (1,128 square km).]

Prior to the discovery of Martinique by Columbus in 1493, the area was inhabited by Arawak and Carib Indians. There was no real European interest in the island until French colonies were established in 1635. Though the British made brief attempts to occupy the island during the 18th and 19th centuries, it has remained under French control ever since (along with Guadeloupe). Slavery was abolished in 1848 and, in the late 19th century, tens of thousands of immigrant workers arrived from India to replace the slave workforce on the plantations. Both Martinique and Guadeloupe were administered as parts of French Antilles. In 1946, rather than following a path to independence, the two islands were incorporated into the French nation with the status of Overseas Departments.

There was little political evolution until 1974 when Martinique, along with Guadeloupe and French Guiana, was granted some local political and economic autonomy. This was increased in 1982 and 1983 following a package of decentralisation policies introduced by French President Mitterand. Most affairs, with the major exceptions of defence and security, are now generally under local control. The thrust of French government policy in the region is now to bolster links between its remaining possessions, Martinique and Guadeloupe, and other French Caribbean nations

Land and Environment

Martinique is about 50 miles (80 km) long and reaches a maximum width of 22 miles (35 km). Among the smallest of the French overseas territories, Martinique has one of the highest population densities in the Antilles.

The north of the island is mountainous and lushly forested. It features 4 ensembles of dramatic pitons and mornes: the Piton Conil on the extreme North, which dominates the Dominica Channel, the Mount Pelee, an active volcano, the Morne Jacob, and the Pitons du Carbet, an ensemble of 5 beautifully shaped, rainforest covered extinct volcanoes dominating the Bay of Fort de France at 1,196 meters. The most dominating of the island's many beautiful mountains, with 1397 meters, is the infamous volcano Mount Pelée. The volcanic ash has created beautiful grey and black sand beaches in the north (in particular between Anse Ceron and Anse des Gallets), contrasting markedly from the white sands of Les Salines in the south.

The south is more easily traversed, though it still features some impressive geographic features. Because it is easier to travel and because of the many beautiful beaches and food throuout this region, the south receives the bulk of the tourist traffic. The beaches from Pointe de Bout, through Diamant (which features right off the coast the beautiful Roche de Diamant), St. Luce, the town of St. Anne all the way down to Les Salines are very popular.

Relief and drainage

The mountainous relief of Martinique takes the form of three principal massifs. These are an active volcano, Mount Pelée, which rises to 4,583 feet

(1,397 metres), to the north; the Carbet Mountains, of which Lacroix Peak reaches 3,923 feet (1,195 metres), in the centre; and Mount Vauclin, rising to 1,654 feet (504 metres), in the south.

The tortuous relief of the island has created a complex drainage pattern characterized by short watercourses. In the south the Salée and Pilote rivers flow down from the slopes of Mount Vauclin. In the centre the rivers flow outward from the Carbet Mountains in a starlike pattern; they include the Lorrain, Galion, Capot, and Lézarde rivers. In the north the Grande, Céron, Roxelane, Pères, and Sèche rivers are little more than irregular torrents.

The northern coastline of Martinique is characterized by steep cliffs; farther south, however, the cliffs become lower. There are two large bays Fort-de-France and Marin on the western coast. Coral reefs, headlands, and coves line the eastern coast.

Climate

The climate is remarkably constant, the average temperature being about 79 °F (26 °C), with average minimums of 68–72 °F (20–22 °C), average maximums of 86–90 °F (30–32 °C), and temperature extremes of 59 °F (15 °C) and 93 °F (34 °C). The northeast trade winds, which blow almost 300 days per year, temper the heat, but winds from the south are hot and humid and sometimes bring hurricanes.

There are two distinct seasons a relatively dry season, which lasts from December to June, and a rainy winter season from July to December. There is abundant precipitation, especially in July and September, but it is irregularly distributed, varying from about 40 inches (1,000 mm) to almost 400 inches (10,000 mm) per year, depending on elevation and landforms.

Plant and animal life

The climate, together with the fertile volcanic soil, produces a luxuriant flora in four vegetational zones: the maritime zone, the lowlands, the former forest zone, and the upper mountain slopes. The maritime zone includes an enormous mangrove swamp, half of which is located in the bay of Fort-de-France. Morning glories, tropical twining herbs, and sea grapes inhabit the beaches. The lowland vegetation zone, extending from the coast to an elevation of about 1,500 feet (460 metres), has ferns and orchids, as well as various trees, including mahogany, white gum, and other species. Above 1,500 feet is the former virgin forest zone, where large trees and bracken are still found. As elevation increases the trees grow smaller. A transitional zone is characterized by peat moss. Above about 3,000 feet (900 metres) the upper slopes are almost bare, except for some stunted forest. Forests cover about one-fourth of the total land area.

There are relatively few kinds of animals on the island. The mongoose was introduced in the 19th century in the hope of eliminating the deadly rat-tailed viper, but the plan was unsuccessful. Also found are manicons (a kind of opossum), wild rabbits, wild pigeons, turtledoves, and ortolans, which are small birds that are often netted and fattened as a table delicacy.

People

The original Carib Indian population disappeared after Europeans arrived, partly as a result of disease, conflicts with the Europeans, and assimilation. In 1658 French settlers on the island numbered about 5,000. Slaves brought from Africa added a further ethnic component. Today people of mixed European and African ancestry account for more than nine-tenths of the population, but the island's economy is largely controlled by the small proportion of people of European descent. A small fraction of the population is descended from labourers brought from the Indian subcontinent. A creole similar to that spoken in Haiti is commonly heard, but French is the official language.

The population of Martinique increased rapidly until the late 1970s, when, plagued by unemployment and other economic maladies, the residents of the island began to emigrate in large numbers to France and in smaller numbers to French Guiana. About one-fourth of the total population lives in Fort-de-France, and nine-tenths of the population lives in urban areas.

Family, Marriage, and Kinship

Marriage. In principle, Martinican couples marry by mutual consent on the basis of love. Particularly in village society, this typically follows a period of premarital co-residence and, frequently, childbirth. Families often apply subtle pressure to ensure that their eligible children "marry up" or at least do not "marry down" in terms of class and, especially, race as measured by skin color. Strong pressures to maintain endogenous family ties are exercised within the béké community. Legal formalities for marriage and divorce are those of France; declarations of common law marriage (concubinage) may be made at town hall. Approximately two thousand marriages are performed yearly in Martinique; between three hundred and four hundred divorces are processed. Little more than one-third of eligible age Martinicans (age 18 for men, age 15 for women) are in fact married.

Domestic Unit. The domestic unit in Martinique has evolved somewhere between the nuclear and extended family. Couples live together with their children without the benefit of formal matrimony, and nearby relatives often assist with child care. Approximately one-third of single mothers are heads of the household and depend on relatives for child care and housework. Feminist challenges notwithstanding, it has been a longstanding practice in Martinican society for men to take mistresses.

Inheritance. Inheritance follows the laws of France. In practice, particularly due to a high frequency of "illegitimate" heirs, following death the division of land and real estate may be subject to dispute and protracted litigation.

Socialization, Etiquette, Religion and Socialization

Socialization

Child Rearing and Education. Child rearing is strict and often includes corporal punishment. In households where the father is present, it is generally he who is in authority. Martinique benefits from the same highly developed child care infrastructure and school system in place in France.

Higher Education. Even before the establishment of the University of the Antilles—French Guiana in Schoelcher pursuing a higher education in France was the goal of upwardly mobile Martinicans. University and professional degrees convey high status in local society. University education and professional training abroad (particularly in France) carry more weight in local eyes than do equivalent educational experiences in Martinique.

Etiquette

Formality and social distancing characterize most interactions between strangers in Martinique. Language is the principal means by which social distance is established and maintained. Even though Creole is the lingua franca it is much more polite to address the other, at least until a sufficiently close relationship is established, in French. It can be considered disrespectful to initiate conversations in public spaces (i.e., government offices, stores) in Creole. If one can speak French, addressing a stranger in Creole is to acknowledge that person as socially inferior. Respecting French language norms of politeness (such as second person usage of the more formal vous as opposed to tu) is also a must. Shaking hands is part of local etiquette.

Informal interactions call for more intimate social exchanges. These include double (and even triple and quadruple) cheek kissing, even between members of the same sex. While double cheek kissing parallels that of French society in its frequency, it is performed in a distinctly Antillean style: more slowly and with greater head turning for a more perpendicular cheek-to-lip encounter.

Religion

Religious Beliefs. Ever since the establishment of French rule Roman Catholicism has been overwhelmingly predominant. In recent years evangelical Protestantism (e.g., Seventh Day Adventists) has been growing in strength as have Jehovah's Witnesses. Bahai, Jewish, and Muslim faiths also have their own sites of religious and cultural congregation.

Throughout and beyond the slave era a parallel system of belief and practice, known as quimbois , has existed alongside Christianity. Quimbois encompasses plant and herb remedies, sorcery, and spiritual healing, and is embedded deep within popular culture. A version of nineteenth century Hinduism, brought to the West Indies by south Indian immigrants, still survives in small temples and shrines where the burning of incense, garlanding of statues, and offering of sacrifices are still practiced. Both Hindus and quimboiseurs ordinarily consider themselves also to be Catholic while the local Rastafarians—a sect that began in Jamaica and worships the late emperor, Haile Selassie—break more squarely with Western religion.

Religious Practitioners. An archbishop presides over forty-seven parishes and over 60 priests.

Rituals and Holy Places. In addition to the regularly celebrated Catholic holidays (Christmas, Easter, All Saints Day, etc.) each commune (district) organizes an annual celebration in the name of a saint or Catholic holiday. Annual local Catholic pilgrimages include Sacré Coeur in Balata, the Way of the Cross of Mount Vauclin, Notre Dame de la Salette in Sainte-Anne and Saint-Michel in François. Notre Dame de la Délivrande, celebrating the 1851 rescue of Martinique's first bishop from a tropical storm in the Atlantic, has become the patron saint of the island as well as the pilgrimage of Morne-Rouge. A number of Martinicans partake in the cult of miraculous medal of Sainte Catherine Labouréin Paris. In recent years there has been annual revival of the Hindu mela .

Death and the Afterlife. Death announcements are a regularly scheduled part of the daily official radio program. Funeral rites invariably follow Roman Catholic practice and, especially in villages, include public funeral processions in which men are uniformly dressed in black suit, white shirt and black tie. Jour des Morts (Day of the Dead), when people gather in cemeteries after dusk to light candles at grave sites, is observed 2 November, the day after All Saints' Day.

Medicine and Health Care

Modern medicine, administered through the Administration of Health and Social Services of France, has supplanted rural medical beliefs and practices relying on herbal cures. Folk or traditional medical practitioners (guérisseurs) are no longer common even in villages. Widespread belief in quimbois (sorcery) and the associated concepts of the evil eye and devil's work has been supplanted by psychiatric and other scientific explanations of extraordinary behavior.

Secular Celebrations

In addition to all the national holidays of France such as Bastille Day, Armistice Day, and May Day, Martinique observes Emancipation Day (marking the end of slavery) and Bannzil Kréyol (the International Day of Creole). Although originally grounded in Catholic ritual (encompassing, in particular, Mardi Gras and Ash Wednesday)

Carnival has become a more secular and boisterous festival. Distinctive and often wild costume and behavior are on display, as groups vie in parade for attention and appreciation. On Mardi Gras regalers dress in red; the following day, in black and white. Music and dance "wake the dead." Vaval, a giant puppet, is the symbol of Carnival, and each year personifies a new theme. Vaval's ritual bonfire at Wednesday dusk marks the end of the raucous festivities.

Arts and the Humanities

Arts Support. Martinique is endowed with an extraordinarily rich infrastructure for the arts: that of the region (FRAC-Regional Funds for Contemporary Art); the municipality of Fort-de-France (SERMAC-Municipal Service of Cultural Action); and mixed national and departmental (CMAC-Martinican Centre of Cultural Action).

Festivals for artists and musicians, competitions and prizes, and concerts and institutional acquisitions support every art genre.

Literature. Explorers and missionaries (Father Labat being the most renowned) introduced seventeenth century Martinique to the world. A rich indigenous oral literature, best represented by the folk tales of the wily rabbit Compère Lapin, developed during the slave and post-slave era. With the publication of Return to My Native Land (1939), AiméCésaire explained négritude (black consciousness of Africa and its West Indian diaspora) to the rest of the world; Edouard Glissant (The Lizard ; Antillean Discourse) followed this genre. Psychiatrist Frantz Fanon provided a penetrating analysis of the French West Indian mentality in Black Skin, White Masks (1952). Contemporary Martinican writers of note include Patrick Chamoiseau (whose novel Texaco won the

Prix Goncourt) and Raphaël Confiant (The Negro and the Admiral).

Graphic Arts. The most notable graphic arts movements are the 1970s Caribbean Negro School, inspired by apprenticeship in Africa following study in France; and the 1980s Fromajé, steeped in the island's ancestral heritage. Annual artistic events are CMAC displays of paintings and sculptors, pastels and watercolors; SERMAC's Festival of Fort-de-France; and expositions by the Association of Young Martinique Artists (ADJAM) and the Martinican Association of Plastic Artists (AMPC). FRAC hosts artists-in-residence and degree-granting training is offered by the Regional School of Plastic Arts of Martinique (ERAPM). Legacies of Carib Indian culture survive in basket weaving and artisinal pottery from the colonial era continues but the Trois-Ilets Pottery has been modernized.

Performance Arts. Around the world Martinique is popularly known for its music, thanks to such groups as Kassav and Compagnie Créole. Zouk has largely supplanted the biguine of the past although the group Malavoi preserves a traditional instrumental style. A distinctive style of drumming is gwo-ka . Theater flourishes, especially at the Municipal Theater and Regional Dramatic Center. The Grand Ballet of Martinique maintains the island's folk heritage, mostly for the tourist audience.

The State of the Physical and Social Sciences

Research institutes of France in Martinique include those for general science and development, geography, agronomy, geology and mineralogy, and oceanography. Demographic and economic studies are conducted through INSEE (National Institute for Statistics and Economic Studies). The

Martinican campus of the University of the Antilles-French Guiana offers two tracks of study: law and economics; and letters and social sciences. Training courses for social work, business and management, and nursing and midwifery are also available.

Social Stratification

Classes and Castes. Universal suffrage and departmentalization (i.e., statehood) have seen the power of the békés shift from politics almost exclusively to economics. Mulattos (mixed-race persons) still retain a residual social edge over those who are descended more directly from exclusively African forebears.

Symbols of Social Stratification. Western dress, urban outlook, white collar employment, and automobile ownership are all traits of social advancement. However, the most direct hallmark of upper class status besides skin color is the use of the French language rather than Creole and a metropolitan accent rather than a West Indian accent.

Gender Roles and Statuses

The Relative Status of Women and Men. Machismo, a long-established tradition within West Indian society, still permeates Martinican society. There is a long matrifocal history of single female-headed households, which since 1975 have been heavily subsidized through government family allowance funds. Women retain power and influence in the private domain but in the more public spheres few women (with some exceptions in the fields of education and culture) occupy positions of high authority. Contraception has created a "fertility revolution," decreasing the child bearing average from almost six children in the 1950s to slightly over two in the 1990s.

Since the 1980s over one-half of Martinican women have entered the workforce, where they are disproportionately represented as salaried employees in the services sector where they are employed as servants, clerical workers, and teachers. Martinican women are three times as underemployed and more unemployed than men. One-fifth of women have achieved middle class economic status. Despite an evolution among the young and middle class, the combination of large numbers of unmarried women in an economy that creates pressure for marriage puts wives in a vulnerable position within the household, where they must often submit to male chauvinistic attitudes and behavior lest their husbands abandon them and/or take mistresses.

Economy

Martinique has a typically Caribbean economy, depending heavily on a few agricultural products and tourism and relying on outside sources, principally France, for aid. A large trade deficit and a high rate of unemployment are major impediments to economic progress. Nevertheless, the island enjoys one of the higher standards of living in the Caribbean, partly due to a wage scale linked to that of metropolitan France.

Agriculture and fishing

The principal agricultural products are sugarcane and bananas, the latter grown chiefly for export. Sugarcane is mainly used to produce rum, which is also exported. Fresh and canned pineapples and pineapple juice, cut flowers, avocados, eggplants, and citrus fruits are other exports. Grown for the domestic market are yams, cassava, sweet potatoes, and breadfruits. Crabs, lobsters, clams, cod, and crayfish are fished mainly for local consumption. The widespread destruction of banana plantations caused by occasional hurricanes has created major setbacks.

Manufacturing

Significant manufactures include cement, processed sugar and rum, clothing, fabricated metals, and yawls and other small craft. There is an important oil refinery at Fort-de-France. Other industries include rum distilling, fish and fruit canning, sugar refining, the processing of cattle feed, soft drinks, and food, and the manufacture of pottery, wooden furniture, and chemicals. The government has promoted light manufacturing, and the construction of yachts and sport boats is of growing importance.

Tourism and trade

One of the most popular tourist areas in the Caribbean, Martinique has a flourishing cruise ship business that brings tourists mainly from France, Canada, and the United States.

Martinique's economy is heavily dependent on trade with France, which provides the majority of the island's imports and exports. The value of imports far surpasses that of exports, resulting in large trade deficits. Exports include agricultural products (significantly bananas), refined petroleum products, and processed foods and beverages (notably rum). Chief imports are agricultural implements and machinery, food, automobiles, mineral fuels, and chemicals and chemical products.

Transportation

Martinique maintains regular air and sea links with France and North America. The main port is Fort-de-France. There is an international airport at Lamentin, to the east of Fort-de-France. An expressway links Fort-de-France with coastal towns. There are local bus services, and small coastal steamers connect various points around the island.

Food in Daily Life. Until supermarkets and imported common cuisine (including steak-and-fries and fast food chains) proliferated, daily

Martinican cuisine was characterized by a unique blend of French and Creole cooking, often laced with piment (hot pepper). Open air markets still supply locally grown fruits (bananas, coconuts, guava, pineapples, mangoes, love apples, and passion fruit) and vegetables (breadfruit, Chinese cabbage, yams, gumbo, and manioc). Much Martinican cuisine is prepared from seafood and shellfish including salted cod, lambi (conch), octopus, blaff (boiled fish with chives) and the national dish, court-bouillon (fish in a spicy tomato sauce). However, one-quarter of the average household food budget is now spent on mostly imported meats and poultry, especially beef. Restaurants have yet to cultivate the same air of sophistication and hospitality as in France

Food Customs at Ceremonial Occasions. Bounding a fat sausage of spicy pig's blood—is a staple at all holidays. At Easter and on Pentecost a spicy dish of crab and rice, matoutou, is always served. Small fried vegetable or fish cakes (acras), used to be reserved for saints days but have become a popular appetizer. Special occasions call for a gumbo and vegetable soup with crab or salted meat (calalou). East Indian influence is evident in the colombo, a mutton, goat, or chicken curry. No social gathering is complete without drinking ati-punch (straight rum with a twist of lemon sweetened with cane sugar) or aplanteur (fruit juice and rum).Shrubb (rum with marinated orange or tangerine rinds) is served at Christmas.

Basic Economy. The economy is linked to that of France. The agricultural basis for the island—banana, sugar, and pineapple plantations—is heavily subsidized by the French economy.

Land Tenure and Property. Nearly one-half of large land holdings were inherited from colonial-era distributions. Land tenancy may be practiced either by share (colonage) or cash (métayage). Land division for inheritance purposes is supposed to follow normal French legal practice but unresolved plot disputes abound.

Commercial Activities. While the agricultural sector employs only about 10 percent of the population, approximately one-third of workers are in government service. Another one-third of the workforce is chronically unemployed.

Major Industries. Sugar cane processing and tourism are the major industries.

Trade. Imports are equal to more than five times exports. Primary imports are consumer goods and agro-industrial products. Major exports are bananas, pineapples, flowers, and rum. Martinique's principal trading partners include metropolitan France, Great Britain, Germany, and Guadeloupe.

Politics

Government and Society

Government. Martinique is one of one hundred departments (states) of the French Republic and one of five overseas departments (DOMs). It sends four deputies (representatives) to the National Assembly in Paris and in turn receives an appointed prefect who serves as the central government's local executive. There are also two locally elected assemblies: the general council with forty-five members, which is responsible for roads, housing, transportation, education and overall infrastructure, and a regional council with forty-one members, which oversees economic, social, sanitary, cultural and scientific development.

Leadership and Political Officials. The establishment and exploitation of patron-client relations are significant means of leadership attainment in this small society. Job and contract distribution is a major criterion for political popularity. Political parties can be classified into three major categories: local affiliates of French parties which are in favor of continued departmental status for Martinique (the Gaullist Rassemblement pour la République, the moderate right Union pour la Démocratie Française, and the leftist Fédération de la Martinique); those advocating autonomy for Martinique within the French Republic (the Parti Communiste Martiniquais, Parti Progressiste Martiniquais); and pro-independence parties (Combat Ouvrier, Conseil National des Comités Populaires, Group Revolution

Socialiste, Mouvement des Démocrates et Ecologistes pour une Martinique Souveraine, Mouvement Indépendantiste Martiniquais). The major figure in twentieth-century Martinican politics is AiméCésaire, founder of the Parti Progressiste Martiniquais.

Social Problems and Control. The legal and judicial systems of Martinique are those of France, as are the police force and gendarmerie. They are accorded high legitimacy in the eyes of the populace. The most common crime is theft, especially car break-ins and automobile theft. Economic and financial crimes are also common. Social and political protest movements have occasionally resulted in fatalities. Politically motivated vandalism has damaged or destroyed monuments and installations at electricity, telecommunications, police, and court offices.

Military Activity. France's armed forces in Martinique are the third strongest military contingent in the Caribbean after the United States and Cuba. Land, sea, and air units are represented as well as the gendarmerie. Over five thousand officers, sailors, and soldiers serve in Martinique and Guadeloupe, most of whom are from France. A special program of "adapted military service" permits Martinican conscripts to remain in the French Antilles, receiving vocational training and contributing to local development.

Social Welfare and Change Programs

Martinicans benefit fully from the generous package of welfare programs available to all French citizens, covering health, retirement, widowhood, and large families. Given the high rate of unemployment in Martinique, the workfare program plays an important role in ensuring a minimal income level for the least privileged. A joint commission made up of members of the general and regional councils controls local economic development. As part of France, Martinique is part of the European community, and has benefitted over the years from development funds made available through the community. In anticipation of the 1992 Treaty of Maastricht creating a single European economic

zone, the European community instituted a special program to ensure that the overseas parts of constituent members not be adversely affected by economic integration.

Nongovernmental Organizations and Other Associations

Local branches of nongovernmental organizations such as Amnesty International, the Red Cross,

Doctors of the World, and Catholic Rescue channel Martinican philanthropy throughout the world.

Justice

The French system of justice is in force. The Court of Appeal at Fort-de-France also has jurisdiction over French Guiana. There are two lower courts (tribunaux d'instance), one higher court (tribunal de grande instance), one administrative court, and a commercial court.

Health and welfare

There are several general and maternity hospitals, as well as some dispensaries. Martinique receives the same social benefits as mainland France.

Education

Education is free and compulsory for children between 6 and 16 years of age. There are primary, secondary, and vocational schools. The vast majority of the people are literate. Higher education is usually pursued in metropolitan France; a number of scholarships are available. The Martinique campus of the University of the Antilles and Guiana is in a suburb of Fort-de-France.

Cultural Life

As an overseas department of France, Martinique's culture blends French and Caribbean influences. The city of Saint-Pierre (destroyed by a volcanic eruption of Mount Pelée), was often referred to as the Paris of the Lesser Antilles. Following traditional French custom, many businesses close at midday, then reopen later in the afternoon. The official language is French, although many Martinicans speak Martinican Creole, a subdivision of Antillean Creole virtually identical to the varieties spoken in neighboring British-speaking islands of Saint Lucia and Dominica. Mostly based on French, Martinique's creole also incorporates a few elements of English, Spanish, Portuguese, and African languages. Originally passed down through oral storytelling traditions, it continues to be used more often in speech than in writing. Its use is predominant within friends and the family cell. Though it is normally not to be used in professional situations, it is being increasingly used in the media and by politicians as a way to redeem national identity and by fear from a complete cultural assimilation by mainland France.

Most of Martinique's population is descended from African slaves brought to work on sugar plantations during the colonial era, generally mixed with some French, Amerindian, Indian (Tamil), Lebanese or Chinese elements. Between 5 to 10% of the population is of Eastern Indian (Tamil) origin. The island also boasts a small Syro-Lebanese community, a small but increasing Chinese community, and the "Beke" community, White descendants from the first French and British settlers, which still dominate parts of the Agricultural and Trade sectors. The Beke people (which total around 5,000 people in the island, most of them of aristocratic origin) generally live in mansions on the Atlantic coast of the island (mostly in the François - Cap Est district). In addition to the island population, the island hosts a metropolitan French community, most of which lives on the island on a temporary basis (generally from 3 to 5 years).

There is an estimated 250.000 people of martinican origin living in mainland France, most of them in the Parisian region.

Today, the island enjoys a higher standard of living than most other Caribbean countries. The finest French products are easily available, from Chanel fashions to Limoges porcelain. Studying in the métropole is common for young adults. For the rest of the French, Martinique has been a vacation hotspot for many years, attracting both upper-class and more budget-conscious travelers.

Martinique has a hybrid cuisine, mixing elements of French, African, and Asian traditions. One of its most famous dishes is the Colombo, a unique curry of chicken(curry chicken), meat or fish with vegetables, spiced with a distinctive masala of Bengali or Tamil origins, acidulated with tamarind and often containing wine, coconut milk, and rum. There is also a strong tradition of créole desserts and cakes, often employing pineapple, rum, and a wide range of local ingredients.

The pre-Lenten Carnival of Fort-de-France, featuring a parade with elaborate masks, is an annual event. Vodou (Voodoo) ceremonies are sometimes held, though they are far less important in Martinique than they are in Haiti. Cockfighting is a popular sport. Sites of historical interest include the Pagerie Museum, the reconstructed birthplace of Empress Joséphine, consort of Napoleon I, in Les Trois-Îlets. Joséphine was born in 1763 to a Martinique planter named Joseph Tascher de La Pagerie.

Martinique: Lifestyle and Tradition

Martinique is a place where tradition is embraced with enthusiasm in every aspect of daily life. Introduced by the many different cultures, European, African, Indian and Caribbean,

The colorful traditional costumes, adherence to religious festivities, the carnivals, zouk music, the boat races of gommiers and yoles...this is Martinique. Enjoying life to its fullest, both discrete and exuberant at the same time, with the soft Caribbean rhythms in concert

One cannot fail to mention the cuisine, which is as indicative of the island as anything else, to be seen and tried...and tried again!

Contact with the locals brings forth a hospitality that is both friendly and respectful. You will often be lured into friendly banter with the locals or enticed to try some traditional punch. you are guaranteed a good time if invited to a local party or festival which occur year round.

The population is made up in great part by black, Creole and mixed races, the 15000 French or "metropolitains" as they are locally known remain in the minority. There continues the immigration of the locally born adults towards France for economic reasons but their attachment to Martinique has not lessened.

Carnival in Martinique

The Antilles' Carnival follows the universal carnival tradition but has a distinctly European flavor.In Martinique carnival festivities commence on the first Sunday after the Epiphany and reach their climax on Shrove Tuesday

In 2017 these 5 days of celebration are from Saturday 25 February to Wednesday 01 March..

The festivities start straight after the Epiphany, that is to say even up to 2 months before Shrove Tuesday. The weekends host street parades, themed events and private celebrations that grow in intensity as the season progresses. The local government and community representatives meet to organize the festivities, every Sunday sees processions throughout the island.Every village elects a Queen and Junior Queen to be carried in triumph at the grand parade. Even the grandmothers compete for the honor, dressing in their finest traditional costumes.

Hidden from prying eyes each village has prepared new costumes and props which are unveiled only for the "vidé" or Carnival Parade which occupies the streets of Fort de France for the 5 days...

During the carnival the daily life of Martinique comes to a stand still and the island comes alive with "Carnival Fever". Preparations start months in advance. During the five days of official celebration many of the younger generations don't sleep, parading by day and partying by night.

The Carnival King, or VAVAL (a satirical mannequin representing a politician, a public figure or an institution), is carried through the streets leading the festival parade. The Carnival Queen , elected from the various villages, is seated beside the Vaval during the parades.

Martinique's most famous musical groups spread out across the island between the parades ensuring the villages are filled with music 24 hours a day and drawing the crowds along in their wake.

The carnival is also an opportunity to show off the traditional masks of the island:The red clay men wear masks covered entirely in red clay, the nègs gwo-sirop, men coated from head to toe in sugar syrup and charcoal (are caricatures of the rebel slaves from Africa in contrast to the native Creole islanders); mariann lapofig, dressed entirely in banana leaves; the moko-zombis are dancers on African inspired trampolines; the guiablesses…mingling in glitzy costumes both the beautiful girls of the island as well as the young men cross-dressing in the abandon of the moment.

During the Vidè the island throbs with pulsing music, tambourines, trumpets and horns are accompanied by steel drums, bamboo sticks even pots and pans become percussion instruments, the rhythms overlapping from Zouk to beguin. There is even a street parade in pigiamas that heads off at 5 am filling the streets of Lamentin with the shuffling of "slippered" feet.The pinnacle of the festivities is during the four days leading up to Ash Wednesday.

Every day has its theme, Saturday and Sunday everyone dresses up as they please, Monday is the day of Burlesque Weddings, men dressed as brides parading on foot, float and brad jak....

Tuesday is the day of the devil: everyone dressed in red and costumed as the devil.

Finally on Ash Wednesday, the day dedicated to the joyeuses pleureuses (devilettes, devils that cry for the death of Vaval), all dressed in black and white of mourning for the death of Vaval, who is symbolically burnt on a bonfire at nightfall.

At the celebration's end the island enters the period of Lent, that leads up to Easter. Lent, the period of fasting and abstinence coincides with the dry season on Martinique. Tradition requires that one does not dance, listen to music and all weddings and other celebrations are postponed until after Lent.

A BIT OF HISTORY

The carnival was first celebrated in Martinique at Saint Pierre by the French Catholics in the 18° century. In the 17° and 18° century it was a celebration reserved for the rich colonies, with elegant receptions in costume.Only after the abolition of Slavery in 1848 the carnival was democratized and adopted its characteristic style, influenced by the former slaves' adaptation of their own beliefs and traditional instruments: tambourines, cha-cha, ti-bois...

The Carnival of Saint Pierre
From 1848 to 1902 the Carnival of Saint Pierre was particularly renowned in Martinique, despite the fact that the celebrations at the time were overshadowed by the discrimination of the time . In effect, one side of the colony was celebrating with masked balls, private banquettes and luxurious costumes whilst the other side of the island was occupied with celebrations of the vidés nègres. After the catastrophe of Saint Pierre, the carnival festivities were halted for 2 years in Martinique. It was upon recommencement that the Carnival relocated its hub to Fort de France.

Gommiers and yoles

The gommier is tradition, sport and enjoyment.We present this truly Antillean product, its historic origins and antique methods of construction.

The construction of the gommier

The Gommier is a traditional vessel, still constructed today using the same techniques and characteristics of its predecessors. Even before Christopher Columbus reached the Antilles there were boats similar to the gommiers used by the inhabitants to move between the islands and for fishing.

The names is derived from Gommier, the tree Gomme or rubber from which the boats are carved

The trunk is cut and hollowed out, softened by the use of fire and then sculpted with water and stone. The cutting of trees is limited and controlled by the National Office of Forests.

The Gommier, or "Dacryodes hexandra" according to its botanic classification, presents two varieties of tree differentiated only by its bark, red and white. The white species has a smooth almost shiny bark whilst the red species has a bark that is wrinkly and cracked. The trunk can become very large and tall though irregular in shape, often folded upon itself.The wood is of a very compact composition and hardy, producing a resin which is water resistant and has and incense like perfume. Naturally, the vessels were given the name of the tree from which they are built.The Red Cedar Cedrella odorata seems to have been the first material used to produce gommier, there are examples of the vessels made from Cedar that resemble Arabic ships. Being a larger tree than the Gommier or Candle tree the Cedar permitted builders to produce larger boats thus transporting more passengers or goods though less maneuverable due to their size. Apart from these two types of tree, the inhabitants of the Caribbean used other varieties of tree to create not only the hull but also fixtures and fittings for the vessels.Taken from the work: "Gommier : le canot caraïbe" by Serge LUCAS

Gommier and Yole

Over time the gommiers were replaced by yoles made from wood.

It is difficult to differentiate between the two types of boat, both are made of wood and are of similar dimensions, from 8 to 10 meters long . With a rectangular sail, a mast made from tropical timber and boom from bamboo both boats typically have a crew of around 10 people.The primary differences between the two vessels are that the skiff unlike the gommier is not carved out of a trunk and that navigation is performed using poles to lean the boat rather than a rudder.

Today, several associations contribute to maintaining the traditional sport alive, both as a tradition and as a sport.Every year approximately

18 regattas for gommiers and skiffs are organized often with large public and media attendance. The most important regattas often have thousands of spectators (75.000 at Schoelcher for the skiff regatta in 2004) and the entire island focuses on the event.The races are truly inspiring given the acrobatics of the crews battling to harness the force of the wind.

In August there is the most important event of the race calendar, the "Tour de la Martinique".

Rum of Martinique

In Martinique you can appreciate a truly special product resulting from years of tradition and passion. Rum the ideal tropical companion in your moments of relaxation and enjoyment, be it in a hammock under a coconut tree or sipping a cocktail at the disco on the beach…... Rum also represents an activity in itself. A day trip to a rum distillery or plantation gives you the opportunity to explore the creole culture and experience some of the atmosphere of lost times

Rum can be considered a symbol of the island. Martinique produces Rhum Agricole, derived from the distilling of raw sugar, pure and unprocessed. This technique differs greatly from the those more commonly used throughout the world often referred to as "industrial rum" due to their use of the molasses derived as a byproduct from the processing of sugar.

Rhum agricole: is obtained by distilling only fermented sugar cane juice. 100Kg of sugar cane produces 10 liters of rhum agricole

Industrial Rum or Traditional Rum: is produced by using the bi product of the sugar refining process, sugar molasses. It is inferior in aroma and flavor and is commonly used in cocktails or cooking. This was the predecessor to Rhum Agricole.

Rhum vieux or Aged Rum: Rhum Agricole allowed to age over at least 3 years in casks of 650L or less. Aged rum from Martinique is amongst the most highly regarded in the world.

Rhum paille: Rhum Agricolo that has been aged for at least 12 months in cask of capacity superior to 650L.

Since November 1996 the Rhum Agricolo from Martinique has benefited from the recognition AOC. This recognition requires the cultivators of the sugar cane and the producers of rum to respect various regulations with regard to type, location and intensity of cane farming as well as the period of fermentation and process of distillation.

Below you will find a list of the principal distilleries:

- ✓ Distillerie Depaz, St. Pierre
- ✓ Trois Rivieres, S.te Luce
- ✓ La Mauny, Rivière Pilote
- ✓ Distillerie Bally, Carbet
- ✓ Rhum Neisson, Carbet
- ✓ J.M., Macouba
- ✓ Saint-Etienne, Gros Morne
- ✓ Saint-James, S.te Marie
- ✓ Hardy Distillerie, Trinité
- ✓ Usine Sucrière du Galion, Trinité
- ✓ Distillerie Dillon, Fort-de-France
- ✓ Distillerie Simon, François
- ✓ Distillerie La Favorite, Lamentin

Nature of Martinique

The nickname "MADININA" or the island of flowers could not be more appropriate. The island radiates color, Hibiscus, Oleander, Rose, Bougainvillea, Orchids and Frangipani to name but a few of the thousands of species of flower supported by the island.

Martinique's abundance of vibrant flowers, vegetation and landscape changes according to the altitude and the microclimate of the different zones.

The mountain peaks and inland ranges are covered in luxurious tropical forest with thickets of Bamboo, Rubber trees, towering hard woods with vines and hanging vegetation.

The more arid southern zone supports a savanna of Cactus, Frangipani, Balsam, Coconut and Acacia...

The gardens and botanical parks offer you the chance to pass hours immersed in stupendous nature and allow you an appreciation of the vast assortment of plant species to be found in the tropics.

In Martinique lives the Manicou (opossum), found often along the edges of the road in the evenings…be careful not to hit one! Commonly found throughout the island are Mangusta, brought to the island during the last century from India to control the mice population that are drawn to the fields of sugar cane.

Anolis lizards are also readily seen in Martinique. The Trigonocefalo Viper, known as the "fer de lance" or "lance of iron", common in Central America, are a shy animal that prefer the tranquility of the forest and are rarely seen by visitors to the island.

On the Ilet Chancel, islet of Robert, still lives an iguana endemic of Lesser Antilles, the Iguana Delicatissima, while at Fort Saint Louis in Fort de France you can see the Iguana Iguana or Green Iguana.

Found only on Martinique is the Migale or Mantou spider. They are harmless to humans but are regarded as the second most beautiful spider in the world.

The placid Creole cows of Martinique occupy the pastures of the island, often in the company of Egrets that alleviate the cows of natural parasites as well as profit from the cows continuous movement of the grass and topsoil, uncovering small animals such as worms and grasshoppers.

The Sucrier and several other varieties of rare bird such as the white breasted Cinclorcenzia and white breasted Mimo make Martinique one of the last places in the world where it is possible to find these near extinct species.

Along the coast of Martinique is not difficult to meet dolphins, who will accompany you during your cruise catamaran.

The sea floor of Martinique enchants with its colorful fish and coral. The seas of the Caribbean are home to such coral fish species as the Cernie , Barracuda, Parrot Fish, Lobster and crustaceans, Turtles, Sea horse and sponges….

The beaches are populated by crabs and other crustaceans, and the mangrove crabs protected by strict hunting rules can reach astounding dimensions.

Tropical fruits
Banana

Both as an ingredient and meal in itself, the banana is used as a base in many of the local dishes and a staple in the diet. The market stalls contain many diverse varieties of banana: pink, yellow, green, as well as many different shapes:ti nain, figue-pomme, figue-rose and bananas jaunes.Bananas are found throughout the island, every Creole garden and the many plantations that populate the island.

Mango

An impressive plant with lush foliage which forms a canopy, there are various types grown on Martinique, each with its own color and texture. The mature fruit can be red, yellow, green and orange with a sweet fibrous pulp. Popular as a juice or an ingredient in ice-cream and sorbet

Pineapple

he season is generally from February to June but you can always find them at the Market stalls and mobile vendors

Guava
Small round, slightly elongated fruit with yellow green skin and a red flesh with small seeds. Used for juice and marmalades they can be found at the market stalls between May and November

Prune de citere
This unique fruit is in season from July to September and can be seen hanging in bunches like oversized grapes. Yellow-green with a smooth skin the flesh has a sweet, acidic flavor, used for local fruit juices.

Carambole
Commonly known as Star Fruit due to the pattern when cut in cross section, this fruit has a fresh and tasty juice.

Bread Fruit
Originally from Asia the fruit is in season from November to June. Utilized primarily as a side dish the mature fruit is boiled, though it can also be grilled, grated or sliced over a salad.

Antilles Apricot
A fruit particular to the Antilles the "Apricot" is a large fruit with a think skin and the perfumed flesh is the color of an apricot. The fruit reaches maturity between June and August.

Water Apple
A small red fruit similar in appearance to an apple they have a white pulp that is extremely rich in water with a delicate, refreshing flavor. Found during the period July-August.

Corossol
Recognizable for it vivid green skin with soft spines this fruit is used in sorbets as juice and fried.

Citrus Fruits

The island produces many types of citrus fruit including sweet and bitter oranges, grapefruit, lemons and mandarine. The season is generally in June and July. Delicious freshly squeezed. The "citron vert" is commonly used in the islands famous rum cocktails.

Pomme cannelle

A plant originally from the Antilles, this globular green fruit contains an aromatic pulpy flesh with a delicate flavor. In season from July to September.

Cacao

Originally from the humid tropical climes of South America Cacao is cultivated in Martinique throughout the hilly regions. A yellow-green fruit when mature the seed is dried and grilled to produce the powder and Cacao Butter. You will also find it at the markets in the form of Cacao Sticks.

History
Early Period

|Carib Indians inhabited the island at the time Christopher Columbus sighted it in 1493. It was not until 1502, on his fourth voyage, that he visited the island, leaving some pigs and goats there. Neglected by the Spaniards, who sought more material rewards than those the island offered, Martinique was occupied in 1635 by a Frenchman, Pierre Bélain, sieur (lord) d'Esnambuc, who established 80 settlers at Fort-Saint-Pierre at the mouth of the Roxelane River. A year later d'Esnambuc, who had fallen ill, entrusted

Martinique to his nephew, Jacques-Dyel du Parquet, who bought the island from the Compagnie des Îles d'Amérique and developed it into a remarkably prosperous colony. In 1654 a group of 250 Dutch Jews, whom Portuguese forces had ousted from Brazil, introduced sugarcane. Cotton was another early introduction. About 1660 the first cacao (the source of chocolate) plantation was established.]

French rule

After the death of du Parquet, his widow governed the island in the name of her children, but her policies were often opposed by the settlers. In 1658 the French king, Louis XIV, resumed sovereignty over the island and paid an indemnity to du Parquet's children. In 1664 the island was placed under the authority of the Compagnie des Indes Occidentales (West Indies Company); in 1674 it was made part of the French crown domain and was administered according to the Pacte Colonial, a body of principles summarized in the statement "The mother country founds and maintains the colonies; the colonies enrich the mother country. " Supplies and slaves were transported to the French Antilles by the Compagnie du Sénégal, founded in 1664; the slave ships called at Martinique before proceeding to Guadeloupe, permitting the colony first choice of the slaves. In 1723 coffee was introduced from Arabia, thus further contributing to the island's prosperity. In 1787 Louis XVI granted Martinique the right to establish a colonial assembly.

At various times Martinique was attacked by foreign fleets. An attack by the Dutch was repulsed in 1674; further assaults by the British were repelled in 1693 and 1759. In 1762, however, the British captured the island, only to return it to

France under the terms of the Treaty of Paris in 1763. The British recaptured it in 1794 and occupied it until 1802; after having been captured once more by the British in 1809, it was definitively restored to France in 1814.

Slave uprisings occurred in 1789, 1815, and 1822. Following the abolition of slavery in 1848, plantation owners imported workers from India and China in order to avoid paying high labour costs. Universal suffrage was proclaimed in 1848 but was abolished under Napoleon III; after 1870 the Third Republic of France restored representation for the island in the French Parliament.

In 1902 the volcanic eruption of Mount Pelée destroyed the town of Saint-Pierre, killing about 30,000 people. During World War II Martinique adhered to the Vichy government of Nazi-occupied

France for three years before rallying to the Free French cause in 1943. In 1946 Martinique was granted the status of a French département, and in 1974 it was made a région.

Developments since World War II

The postwar politics of Martinique, which was more vociferous in its demands for independence than Guadeloupe, was influenced by Aimé Césaire, the Martinican writer who was one of the founders of the Negritude movement. Césaire, first elected as a deputy in 1946, had originally been a member of the Communist Party, but by 1956 he had resigned and formed his own party, the Progressive Party of Martinique. In 1957 Césaire's party won the Martinican elections by an enormous margin, and it seemed that independence would be achieved.

Martinique's economy was depressed, however, and massive unemployment worked against the independence movement. Emigration to France and French foreign aid had always been palliatives for Martinique's economic problems, and demands for independence resulted only in Martinique's being given greater autonomy. Unrest continued, and by the late 1970s the French government, in an apparent about-face, decided to help Martinique become economically self-sufficient in preparation for independence. Economic problems were exacerbated by the widespread destruction from hurricanes in 1979 and 1980.

Liberation groups were responsible in the 1980s for several bombings in Paris and the French Caribbean islands. Some movement toward autonomy came with France's decentralization law of 1982, under which executive power in the overseas départements devolved from the appointed prefect to the locally elected legislative councils. Over the next several years the local councils also gained greater control over the economy, police, and taxation. After 1986, pro-independence parties won progressively more seats on the legislative councils, in part because of apprehension over France's and thus Martinique's joining the European Union (EU). Although a plurality of the island's voters approved the Treaty on European Union in 1992, less than one-fourth of the electorate participated in the election. A subsequent wave of protests and work stoppages swept the island over fears that Martinique's farms and industries would lose the special protections they had enjoyed under French rule.

In 1999 and 2000 the presidents of the Regional Councils of Martinique, Guadeloupe, and French Guiana proposed and France's Parliament subsequently approved a number of institutional and economic changes for the overseas départements, such as establishing congresses of the Regional and General Councils and granting greater autonomy in international relations. As part of a general reclassification of French overseas possessions in January 2007, Martinique received the combined designation of overseas département and région (DOM-ROM). In January 2010 voters in Martinique and French Guiana rejected proposals that would have moved both départements toward greater autonomy. In another referendum later that month, Martinican voters decided in favour of combining the two councils into one Executive Council. In addition, Martinique's political status was to change from overseas département to territorial collectivity. The changeover was finalized in December 2015. A single local head of government, the president of the Executive Council, replaced the heads of the former two councils to govern alongside the prefect appointed by France.

Alignment in more Detail

__Identification.__ Early in his exploration of the New World, the Amerindian inhabitants of Cuba and Hispaniola told Christopher Columbus about a smaller island which they called Martinino. Coming to the island in 1502, Columbus gave it the name Martinique. Indigenous Carib islanders called it Madiana or Madinina ("Island of Flowers"), designations still used informally in song and poetry. The Carib Indians of Martinique, however, were eradicated by the French in the seventeenth century and ensuing Martinican history and culture has been the result of creolization between

French colonial and African slave societies. Martinicans are French citizens.

Location and Geography. *Situated in the Lesser Antilles of the Windward Islands in the Caribbean, with the islands of Dominica to the north and Saint Lucia to the south, Martinique measures 431 square miles (1,120 square kilometers). It is a mountainous, tropical island of volcanic origin. The 1902 explosion of Mount Pelée totally destroyed the major town of Saint Pierre resulting in the capital being relocated to Fort-de-France.*

Demography. *As of July 1998 the population of Martinique was estimated at 407,284. Another 30 percent of Martinicans currently reside in France. Almost half as many people are born in France of*

Martinican parents as there are residents of Martinique itself. About 5 percent of the population residing in Martinique hail from France. Only about 2,500 Martinicans on the island are direct descendants of the original French settlers (békés). Most of the fewer than five thousand resident foreigners are agricultural laborers from other Caribbean islands.

Linguistic Affiliation. *As part of France, the official language of Martinique for its government, schools, newspapers, and media is French. However, the vernacular which is spoken in most informal and family contexts is Creole. Derived mostly from French (with sprinklings from African, Amerindian, and English dialects), Creole is particularly expressive and idiomatic, using a relatively simple grammatical structure.*

Creole originally developed out of the need for African slaves to communicate among themselves as well as to understand the commands of their French masters. The lack of local Creole literature has prompted many Martinicans to deny that Creole constitutes a language. In Martinique itself, Creole is becoming more and more French as a result of increasing cultural influences from France. Standard French is widely spoken, albeit in a distinctive, lilting French West Indian accent.

Symbolism. *Ile aux Flours ("Island of Flowers") is one of the island's unofficial nicknames; the other, invoking its magical charm, is Pays des Revenants ("Land to Which One Returns"). Thegommier (wooden fishing boat) symbolizes a society surrounded by the sea while the bakoua (a* *high conical hat woven from the pandanus plant) represents the early predominant peasant culture. Colibri (hummingbird) is the island mascot.*

Colorful, striped female dress (madras) with a knotted kerchief represents the languorous West Indian woman of the past. Music and dance, especially of a sensuous variety, are distinctly Martinican. Poets and writers have used the mangrove (swamp) as metaphor for Martinique.

Recently, symbolism has been used to commemorate emancipation from slavery. Initially,

credit for the abolition of slavery had gone exclusively to Victor Schoelcher, the "Abraham Lincoln" of the French colonies. In the last two decades Martinican nationalists have campaigned to emphasize the role of slave revolts and marronage (escape) in their actual liberation. The combined French and Caribbean Martinican identity has created a complex political symbolism that celebrates the French Bastille Day as well as the Martinican abolition of slavery.

Metissage, the mixing of multiple races and ethnicities (particularly French and African but also East Indian and Chinese) into a composite, multi-racial society, includes the controversial concepts ofnégritude (black consciousness),antillanité (West Indianness), and créolité (transcultural fusing with a Caribbean emphasis). Doudouism the image of a tropical island paradise with a French accent, laced with romance and lassitude usually is regarded as a saccharine stereotype]

Urbanism, Architecture, and the Use of Space

Departmentalization and concomitant economic change have transformed the rural sugar plantation character of the island into one highly dependent on the tertiary sector and urban activity. One-third of the island's population converges daily into Fort-de-France, whose narrow symmetrically squared streets are as congested during the day as they are empty at night. Distinctive colonial-era architecture adapted to the tropics wood and stone constructions of large, open spaces with verandas and light filtering (but wind porous) windows is gradually giving way to more "functional," enclosed, air-conditioned construction. Such architectural change, especially in government buildings, projects a less colonial look and feel in favor of a more uniform and efficient French model. An unwalled, conical straw shelter the carbet still dots the landscape and is reminiscent of Amerindian days.

In addition to the classic war memorials which dot villages throughout France (and therefore Martinique), monuments to Victor Schoelcher, the leader of the abolitionist movement, are also common. One monument in particular a statue in the Savanna (central park) of the Fort-de-France of the Empress Josephine, the Martinique-born wife of Napoleon Bonaparte has been the object of continuous vandalism for those who see it as a symbol of racism and continued colonialism (Napoleon's decision to reinstate slavery is attributed to the influence of Josephine).

Dominic Hussain

Travel and Tourism
Travel guide to Martinique

The "Flower of the Caribbean" in the island group called the Lesser Antilles, Martinique is celebrated for its natural beauty. Flowers grown on the island include hibiscus, frangipani and bougainvillea. Surrounded by amazing white sandy coastline and enticing warm waters, the island is a beach lover's paradise.

Being a tropical island with clear blue seas, water sports on Martinique are a popular draw for visitors, who take part in awesome dives around the reefs and underwater shipwrecks. Boating and fishing excursions are popular, as is jet skiing, surfing and water skiing. The island itself is a haven for nature lovers with good hiking opportunities up to volcanic peaks or canyoning around the coastline.

An intriguing element to discover about Martinique is that it is officially an overseas department of France, and offers French culture akin to stepping right into Paris, albeit with a sunnier and less crowded feel. Gourmet French food is abundant, alongside typically Caribbean Creole. As a result of the French influence, Martinique experiences one of the highest standards of living in the Caribbean with modern conveniences and accommodations available.

The north facing Atlantic coast offers the best surf, and it is this part of the island where you will find Martinique's tallest peak, an active volcano called

Mount Pelee. Hiking and canyoning in this area are popular, as is enjoying the magnificent beaches. Many people are drawn to Martinique because of its nightlife, and the southern tourist town of Trois-Ilets provides several bars, nightclubs and casinos to let your hair down.

Martinique Aimé Césaire International Airport is in the capital city of Fort de France. From here it is possible to rent a car, which is a very good way to getting around the island since the road network is well developed. Many visitors also use the short ferry service between Fort de France and the lively resort town of Trois-Ilets to get between the two busiest places.

Tourist attractions

- ✓ Relax on one of the finest beaches in the Caribbean, with white sands and enticing warm waters at Les Salines

- ✓ Go snorkeling or diving in the clear blue Caribbean Sea to discover a magnificent underwater world

- ✓ Challenge the high seas with a boat or fishing excursion off the coast of Martinique on a yacht charter

- ✓ Discover why the island is fondly known as the "Flower of the Caribbean" by visiting the majestic Balata Botanical Gardens

- ✓ Visit the historic town of Sainte-Anne, the "Paris of the Caribbean," and learn more about famous volcanic eruptions from nearby Mount Pelee

- ✓ Live the high life and treat yourself at one of Martinique's prestigious casinos at Trois-Ilets

- ✓ Endulge in genuine French food and wine, while shopping for perfume and Parisian fashion

Travel Tips

Language

French is the dominant language of Martinique, with a local dialect called "Creole patois" also spoken by some inhabitants. English may be used in tourist areas by hotel staff and guides.

Currency

Martinique is an overseas department of France and so it uses the same currency which is the Euro. Some hotels and restaurants will accept US dollars, although stores will not, and it is best to get Euros for cash transactions. The most favorable exchange rates are offered at banks, which are all French owned. There are also plenty of ATMsacross

Martinique. Credit cards are widely accepted for larger purchases in hotels, restaurants and stores.

Time
The time zone in Martinique is GMT-4.

Electricity
Electricity in Martinique runs at 220-240 V/50 Hz variable. You may need a transformer if your electrical appliance differs (most North American electronics run at 110-120 volts). They use a two-pronged rounded European style plug so you will need an adapter for all other style plugs. Sometimes the sockets will accept a third grounding pin which is featured on some electrical plugs, although it is best to travel with a converter just in case.

Communications
The international calling code for Martinique is +596. Cell phone service is exceptionally good in

populated areas, although you may not get much coverage in the more remote areas. There are several phone booths located in cities and towns. The island has an excellent internet network, and the majority of hotels will offer free Wi-Fi, which is also available in the country's airport.

Duty-free

Duty Free goods can be purchased at Martinique Aimé Césaire International Airport. If you are traveling to the US, you are allowed to import one liter of alcohol and 200 cigarettes, 50 cigars or 4 lbs of tobacco.

Things you can do in Martinique

Martinique is a tropical Caribbean island with immaculate sandy beaches and crystal clear waters making diving and snorkeling immensely popular. There are plenty of opportunities atop the water too, with surfing, water skiing and kite boarding on offer. Charter a yacht for a fishing excursion or just a lovely cruise along the sea.

There are plenty of ways to enjoy Martinique on dry land, and trekking offers an alternative perspective of the country. The island is volcanic in origin, with many peaks to climb and shorelines to walk along. Along your hike you can take in the country's endemic wildlife, its famously beautiful hibiscus, frangipani and bougainvillea flowers and great birding opportunities. Getting around is easy with a rental car.

The sea off the coast of Saint-Pierre offers excellent scuba diving sites. *Acquasud* arranges excursions around Le Diamant to shipwrecks and coral reef. Full training and equipment is provided, although you will need to produce a medical certificate. The company also offers snorkeling trips to similar locations.

The north Atlantic facing coast of Martinique is known for its surfing. The best season for northeastern swells is between November and March. *Bliss* based in the town of Tartane, can rent you boards and offers lessons. Another way to experience the waves is by kite surfing. *Fun Caraibes* offer equipment and training.

The coast around Tartane is also popular for waterskiing and jet-skiing. You can arrange trips from *Atlantic Jet Wake*. Or if you would rather paddle around Martinique, try your hand at kayaking with *Caraibe Coast Kayak*.

To rent a larger boat, *A Fleur d'Eau* arranges yacht charters and powerboats, a great ways to explore the Caribbean. If you would rather let someone else be skipper, you can contact *Boucaniers Boating* for a game fishing excursion.

On the island itself, trekking is a fun way to spend the day. *Bureau de la Randonnee* provide hiking trips around Martinique and canyoning around the craggy coast. For nature treks and wildlife spotting, *Bird Quest Tours* provides experienced guides and set itineraries.

Many people enjoy the thrill of quad biking around the rough terrain of the islands interior. *E-Discover* offers group tours suitable for beginners. For a slower paced adventure, horseback riding around Martinique via *Martinique Equitation* is also popular.

Attractions

A tropical island known as the "Flower of the Caribbean," it should come as no surprise that the sheer beauty of Martinique provides a majority of the attractions. You will find some of the best sandy beaches in the world and clear blue waters swathed by palm trees. Martinique also offers a slice of Creole history in the town of Sainte-Anne, and the site of one of the worst natural disasters in the 20th century at Saint-Pierre. Nature lovers will not be disappointed at Balata Botanical Gardens. where a plethora of tropical plantlife is on display.

Sainte-Anne and Les Salines

Sainte-Anne is well known for its superb white sand beaches, including the most famous at Les Salines. It is the idyllic paradise, palm tree lined escape you dream about, complete with enticing clear blue waters to swim in. The town itself is very picturesque, containing quaint Creole housing. Many visitors also chose to stay overnight to unwind after the sun goes down, taking the opportunity to dine in one of the many seafood restaurants.

Address: Sainte-Anne, southeastern Martinique

Website: http://www.sainteanne-martinique.fr/EN/

Saint-Pierre and Mount Pelee

Mount Pelee is an active volcano in the far north of Martinique. In 1902 it erupted, wiping out the entire town of Saint-Pierre and killing 30,000 people, making it one of the most devastating natural disasters of the 20th century. Prior to the eruption, Saint-Pierre was the most important town in Martinique both culturally and economically, and was known as the "Paris of the Caribbean." The town was never restored to its former glory, and there are many historic remains to be seen. To learn more about Mount Pelee, you can visit the Volcanological Museum in town.

Address: Saint-Pierre, north Martinique

Website: http://www.zananas-martinique.com/en-saint-pierre-martinique/

Le Diamant and Diamond Rock

Le Diamant has marvelous beaches, although many visitors come to see Diamond Rock, a small uninhabited island about two miles off the coast. The island was formed by volcanic activity and juts out of the sea at 175 ft tall. It was an important vantage point during the Napoleonic Wars between the French and British in the 19th century, and today holds ecological importance since it is considered to be the last refuge of the Couresse snake, an endemic species to Martinique. Visitors to Le Diamant can swim or dive in the waters, or take a boat trip to the Rock.

Address: Le Diamant, southwest Martinique

Website: http://www.lediamant.fr/

Le Carbet

Le Carbet is a historic fishing town located in the northwest portion of Martinique, home to tranquil beaches and a good place to learn more about life on a Caribbean island. There is an old shipwreck in the water about 650 ft from the coast which can easily be seen on a snorkeling trip. The town is also home to a waterpark called Aqwaland, which makes for a fun day outing and an opportunity to cool off in one of the pools or slides.

Address: Le Carbet, northwestern Martinique

Website: http://www.carbet-martinique.fr/EN/

Balata Botanical Gardens

Celebrated for its flora and fauna, it is no surprise that one of the finest botanical gardens in the world is located in Martinique. The park was opened in 1986 and features over 3,000 varieties of tropical plants. Set on formidable grounds, it is an impressive and peaceful setting six miles from Fort de France. The gardens are open daily between 9:00 a.m. and 6:00 p.m and there is a small admission fee.

Address: Balata Botanical Gardens, central Martinique

Phone: +11-596-644-873

Website: http://www.jardindebalata.fr (French only)

Trois-Ilets

Trois-Ilets is a lively tourist town across the bay from the capital, accessible by a 30 minute ferry ride from Fort de France. Many visitors choose to stay here since it offers many conveniences. By day there are water sports and pretty beaches and by night some of the best restaurants and nightlife in Martinique. The town was also the birthplace of the wife of Napoleon Bonaparte, the Empress of France and you can visit where she was born.

Holidays and Festivals

Links to France remain strong, and thus the Martinique holidays usually coincide. Bastille Day, celebrating the formation of the French Republic, is a public holiday in Martinique. For more French flare, many enjoy Martinique's Beaujolais "nouveau" celebrations in November, heralding the arrival of the first harvest of the grape which makes a punchy and fresh red wine. But true Caribbean spirit is not amiss in Martinique, and the biggest festival of the year is the four day event known as "Vaval," which is similar to Mardi Gras carnivals around the world.

Vaval

This event is known as Carnaval elsewhere in the Caribbean, and Mardi-Gras in many other places, Vaval is held in February every year, concluding on the first day of Christian Lent. Like many similar festivities throughout the world, the event sees four days of masquerades, parades, dancing and music. It is an extremely fun, island-wide party.

Bastille Day.

Bastille Day is a national holiday that commemorates the formation of the French Republic in 1789 after the French Revolution. Many retail stores are closed as families gather to celebrate. It is held annually on July 14.

Le Tour de Martinique

Similar to the "Tour de France," this an annual cycling race is held in Martinique in July. Many roads are closed to accommodate the professional cyclists who come from around the world to compete. The tour reaches most parts of the island, and offers good opportunities as a spectator for sports fanatics.

Tour de Yoles Rondes

Held each year in August, this is the biggest boating event in Martinique. Sailors must use a traditional fishing yacht to compete in several stages around the island. The event attracts many spectators, some choosing to follow the race on the sea by boat. At the end of the day, the event concludes with carnival-style partying.

Beaujolais Nouveau Celebrations

At midnight on the third Thursday of November, the arrival of the new season of Beaujolais red wine is celebrated on the island. Many restaurants and cafes around Martinique will stay open late to appreciate the new wine in a festive atmosphere.

Martinique Jazz Festival

The Caribbean's longest running jazz festival, many international musicians come to Martinique to showcase their talents. It is a 10-day event beginning the last week of November that runs through the first weekend of December.

Food and Restaurants

Martinique has a hybrid cuisine consisting of elements from Africa, France, Carib Amerindian, and South Asia. Its Indian "Tamil" population (which makes up 5-10 percent of the residents), is the source of one of the most famous dishes called *Colombo,* a curry spiced with *masala* (a mix of Indian spices, garlic and ginger) that is flavored with *tamarind* (a tropical pod fruit originating from Africa), and cooked with wine, rum and coconut milk. Creole dishes feature a variety of seafood cooked with spices and local ingredients such as *breadfruit*, *cassava* and *christophine* (similar to a cucumber). French food is extremely popular, as well, and restaurants continually exceed expectations.

Bars and Pubbing in Martinique

The majority of bars and nightclubs in Martinique are located in the capital, Fort de France, which offers a variety of music including Zouk, Reggae, Salsa, Jazz, Hip Hop, and Techno. For a relaxing atmosphere to unwind over a cocktail, you can head to *Bar 'Oc* (97 Route de Didier, Fort de France) before continuing your night out. Another good downtown bar is *L'Appart* (6 Rue Papian du Pont, Fort de France), which offers live music Tuesday through Saturday, 6:00 p.m. until midnight.

There are a few nightclub options in Martinique, such as *Maximus* (Point de Californie, Basse Gondeau), open Monday to Saturday between 7 p.m. and 4 a.m. *Top* nightclub (Zone du Bac, Trinite) or *Zipp's* (Dumaine, Le Francios) are other venues with late night dancing. *May Day Lounge Bar* (Port de Plaisance Bâtiment D2, Le Marin) offers a happy medium between lounge and club, and is open from 10:00 p.m. until 2:00 a.m. Tuesday to Saturday, with salsa dancing and live music on Friday nights. No bars or clubs are open on Sundays.

There are a number of casinos in Martinique, and a night out gambling is a popular pastime. *Casino Bateliere Plaza* (Rue de Alizes, Schoelcher) has two roulette tables, four black jack tables, four poker tables, and 140 slot machines; open until 3:00 a.m. *Casino de Trois-Ilets* (Pointe du Bout, Les Trois Ilets) is another option, with two black jack tables, two poker tables, a craps table, and 70 slot machines; also open until 3:00 a.m.

Dining and Cuisine in Martinique

There are restaurants located all over the Martinique, many of which are in Fort de France or Trois-Ilets, but there are certainly options elsewhere on the island. For Creole food, *La Bredas* (Saint Joseph, Fort de France) is open between 7:30 p.m. and 11:30 p.m., Tuesday through Saturday. Also offering French fare on the menu, you may see dishes like *coiba* (a local seafish) served with *yam* (a type of cassava) cooked in *Maidera* (a fortified wine) sauce.

In Trois-Ilets, head to *Au Poisson s'Or* (12 Rue des Bougainvilliers, Trois-Ilets), specializing in fish and seafood. It is open for lunch 12:00 p.m. to 2:00 p.m., and dinner 7:00 p.m. to 9:30 p.m. Reservations are highly recommended. Another place for Creole in Trois-Ilets is *La Villa Creole* (18 Rue des Anthuriums, Trois-Ilets), which offers typical cuisine such as *boudin* (sausage) and *feroce* (pate made from fresh avocados, codfish and manioc flour). They are open for lunch from noon until 2:00 p.m., and for dinner from 7:00 p.m. until 10:30 p.m. Reservations are also recommended.

A French Overseas Territory, it is no wonder that Martinique's cuisine is so rich and delicious. One of the most popular restaurants is *Le Dome* (Avenue de Arawaks, Fort de France), which provides modern décor and a magnificent view of the adjacent coastline. It is open daily between 12:30 p.m. and 2:00 p.m., and 7:30 p.m. to 10:00 p.m. In Trois-Ilets, *Fleur de Sel* (27 Avenue de l'Imperatrice Josephine, Les Trois-Ilets), also offers tasty French fare alongside Creole and international dishes. It is open Monday to Saturday between 7:30 p.m. and 11:00 p.m.

Shopping and Leisure

Visitors to Martinique will find inexpensive French products such as perfume and fragrances, designer clothes, and wine. In addition, certain luxury items are offered at a 20 percent discount if paying with certain credit cards or travelers checks. Select stores in Fort-de-France offer duty-free shopping or you can save your big haul for the airport (if you're not traveling to EU member states). For perfume or fashion, head to one of the shopping centers such as Galeries Lafayette, Galerie Saint-Louis or Centre Commercial le Rond Point, all in Fort-de-France.

If you're in search of locally produced souviners, there are many artisanal "bijoux Creole" goods. Items include locally crafted jewelry, straw weavings, dolls, pottery, and tapestry. Creole jewelry is steeped in Martinique history, and will easily fit into your luggage to take home. Items include a multi-strand beaded necklaces called *collier chou*, or a cable necklace called a *chaine forcat*. You will be able to find local jewelry in many stores in Martinique or you can head to La Galeria in Le Lamentin, which is home to about 140 boutiques.

To purchase straw baskets, the *Cooperative de Vannerie* in Sainte Marie offers hand woven products. For other handmade items, the main market in Fort de France, Le Grand Marche, is a good place to start. Here you will find local spices, homemade liquors, dolls, and other souvenirs. If you're into collectibles, *La Maison de la Poupee* (literally translated to the "Doll House") is a cool place to see creations utilizing over 600 different types of fronds, leaves and plant materials. The store is located near Bass-Pointe in the far north of the island.

Art is another good buy in Martinique and *Galerie Jecy* in Les Trois-Ilets offers metalwork designed with island themes like starfish, octopus, geckos, and billfish. Les Tros-Ilets has more arts and crafts available at *Le Domaine de Chateau Gaillard*, which features pottery and tapestries. For something very unique, *Les Coraux de Leonne* is a store specializing in art made from coral and other sea materials located in Trinite.

Transportation

Martinique Taxis and Car Rental

Taxis are readily available from Fort de France and the airport to places around Martinique. They do not come cheap, and fares are further increased between 8 pm and 6 am, all day on Sunday, and public holidays, with a 40 percent surcharge. Cabs are available 24 hours a day via *Radio Taxis* (0596-631-010) or *Martinique Taxi*(0596-636-362).

Considering the high standards of the road network, renting a car is a great way to get around and see the beauty of Martinique. You can rent vehicles from Avis (+11-596-421-100), Budget (+11-596-636-362) or Hertz (+11-590-892-805), who all have offices at the airport in Fort de France and other popular locations.

Martinique Water Taxis

There is a shuttle boat which runs between Fort de France, Trois-Ilets and Pointe du Bout. The journey takes about 30 minutes to Trois-Ilets, and slightly less to Pointe du Bout, which is a pleasant way to see the bay, while also avoiding road traffic. There are three companies that offer the service: *Somatours Vedettes* (+11-590-730-553) runs the Fort de France to Pointe du Bout route daily between 6:30 a.m. and 5:15 p.m, departing every hour. Also running the Pointe du Bout route is *Vedettes Madinna* (+11-590-630-646) from 6:20 a.m. until 6:30 p.m. every day. For Trois-Ilets, *Matinik Cruise* line run a scheduled ferry departing every 75 minutes between 6:10 a.m. and 5:45 p.m. There is no service on Sundays.

Martinique Trains and Buses

No rail network exists in Martinique. There are some large public buses, although most are mini-vans marked "TC," which stands for *Taxi Collectifs* (collective taxis). Destinations are marked on a board displayed in the front window. The bus depot in Fort de France is located in Pointe Simon just west of the harbor, and other bus stops are marked with "arret autobus" and normally consist of a blue square with a picture of a white bus. There are no schedules and buses run on demand, usually only departing when full in capacity. Buses run early in the morning and usually end aroudn 6:00 p.m. or 1:00 p.m. on Saturdays. Services on Sundays is extremely limited.

Airports

Martinique Aimé Césaire International Airport

Aime Cesaire is Martinique's only airport, serving flights to USA, Canada, Europe, Latin America, and other Caribbean countries. American Airlines fly to Martinique, with a connection in Puerto Rico, a two hour flight. Air Canada flies direct from Montreal. Air France have several flights to France, including Paris.

The airport is used to catering for a high volume of tourists during peak season, and has many services. There are restaurants and bars, souvenir and gift stores, and duty-free stores (note duty-free will not apply for travelers going to EU destinations). There are two hotels located on site at the airport. There are several car rental agencies at the airport, or there are taxis readily available to take you downtown. The airport is seven miles east of Fort-de-France, about a fifteen minute taxi ride. There is no public transport to and from the airport.

Getting around on Martinique

Public transport in Martinique is very limited, which could explain the reason why there are more cars registered in Martinique per person than anywhere else in France.

Despite the traffic, if you are going to make the most of your stay in Martinique, it is recommended that you hire a car. Without a car you will miss some of Martinique's best landscapes and scenery.

Due to the Taxi Union demands, there is no public transport from the airport, which means that you can either hire a car or take a taxi.

Taxis in Martinique are not cheap. The taxi fare from the airport to Fort-de-France is around €20, €38 to Pointe du Bout and Le Francois and €55 to Sainte-Anne. Be warned that taxis operate an extortionate 40% surcharge between 8PM and 6AM as well as on Sundays and public holidays. To call a taxi 24hrs dial 0596 63 10 10 or 0596 63 63 62.

Buses There are very few buses in Martinique. Most bus services are mini buses marked "TC", which stands for "Taxi Collectifs". The destinations of the buses are marked on a board either on the front window or on the side door. Bus stops (arret autobus) are normally a square blue sign with a picture of a bus in white. Most Taxi Collectifs depart and arrive at the Taxi Collectif Terminal at Pointe Sinon in Fort-de-France. They cost approximately €5 to Saint-Pierre, Pointe du Bout and Diamant, €7 to Sainte-Anne and €9 to Grand-Rivière. There are no timetables and the service can be unreliable. Most services are finished by 6PM weekdays and 1PM on Saturday. There are no services on Sundays.

Shuttle Boats There are shuttle boats every 30mins from Pointe du Bout and Trois Ilet to Fort-de-France. It is a very pleasant way of getting to Fort-de-France and also avoids the traffic. Services finish between 5:45 and 8PM depending upon the day.

Hitchhiking Hitchhiking is very common in Martinique, although like anywhere in the world not recommended. If you are going to hitchhike, take lots of water and try to stay out of the sun. There are very few footpaths in Martinique, so be careful and take the usual precautions that you have to take when hitchhiking anywhere. If you are unsure about getting into a car, just keep walking or wait for another car.

Driving in Martinique Driving in Martinique will be a pleasure in comparison to other Caribbean islands. The majority of roads are of an excellent standard. However, roads in the center of the island go through terrain that can be very steep and caution is advised when rounding the frequent curves.

Your driving license from your home country is valid in Martinique. Driving laws are the same as in France and you have to drive on the right hand side of the road. Distances and speed limits are in Km and Km/h. There are several speed cameras on the island and the Gendarmerie are carrying out an increasing number of speed checks, so you should always watch your speed. Unless otherwise stated, the speed limit is generally 50km/h in towns, 90km/h on major roads and 110km/h on the autoroute between the airport and Fort-de-France. If you rented your car, the rental car firm will charge you 20€ to 25€ for each inquiry of a driver's address by the police in reference to a car receiving a speeding ticket.

When traveling to the airport during rush hours, allow plenty of time. The N5 and Lamentin can get very busy. It is particularly busy between 06:30 and 09:30 and between 15:30 and 18:30.

Buying, Eating and Drinking
Buying
Martinique is a dependent territory of France and uses the euro as currency. US dollars and Eastern Caribbean dollars are not accepted in shops, but

some stores and many restaurants and hotels take credit cards. The best exchange rates can be had at banks. Not all banks will do foreign exchanges and may direct you to Fort De France to do such transactions.

Reportedly, the best offerings include French luxury imports (e.g., perfumes, fashions, wines) and items made on the island, e.g., spices and rum. And some merchants offer 20 percent tax refunds for purchases made by credit card or travelers' checks, though many may not accept the latter.

Shopping opportunities include:

- ✓ Galleria, in Lamentin (near airport), is the island's largest mall, with several European branded stores and others.

- ✓ Fort-de-France's Spice Market offers stalls full of local/unique flowers, fresh fruit and vegetables, and herbs and spices.

- ✓ Rue Victor Hugo...Fort-de-France's main shopping street...a strip of sometimes tiny, Paris-like boutiques, island shops and vendors of fresh fruit and flowers

As a decidedly Catholic island, very few stores are open on Sundays or holidays celebrated in France.

Business hours: Sundays may find many stores closed. Check in-advance before hiring transport to any particular store or shopping area.

Eating

Martinique is unique in contrast to the majority of the other Caribbean islands in that it has a wide variety of dining options. The Gourmet Martinique (2000) lists 456 cafés and/or restaurants on the island – not including the various bars some of which serve food as well as alcohol. The 1998 brochure produced and published by the ARDTM counts up to 500 food-service related establishments (this corresponds to over 3,000 jobs). Restaurants in Martinique range from the exclusive high-end gourmet restaurants to the crêpes, accras, boudin, fruit juices, and coconut milk one can purchase from food merchants on the beach or at snack stands/restaurants in town.

The abundance of both Créole and French restaurants reflects the predominance not only of French tourists in Martinique but also of the island's status as a French DOM. There has been a growing interest in the traditional dishes of the island, and therefore, a more recent profusion of the number of Créole restaurants. Many of the restaurants tailor their menus to cater to both Créole and French tastes

In the 2000 edition of Délices de la Martinique (Delights of Martinique), the guide put together by the island's restaurant union, the editorial given by the then Prefect and director of tourism, Philippe Boisadam, describes the contribution that 'Martinique's cuisine makes to the culinary arts.' Olivier Besnard, the commercial director of the long-haul airline division of Air Liberté, wrote the preface to this same edition. He states that this Créole restaurant and recipe guide is 'a tourist souvenir that you are welcome to take home with you.' Francis Delage, a culinary consultant who assembled most of the recipes for this guide underlines the fact that the island's restaurateurs are the gastronomic ambassadors of Martinique and that they in particular represent the 'quality of the welcome,' 'the products' and 'the savoir-faire of Créole cuisine, which is truly part of France's culinary heritage.'

The changes in tourist composition (behavior, interest) may very well account for the evolution in the culinary offerings in many of today's restaurants. Restaurants in Martinique offer not only French and other International cuisines , but also the possibility of consuming the foods that the Other eats. In this case, the Other refers to the Martiniquais. Visitors can catch a glimpse of the behind the scenes reality regarding Martinique culinary practices through an 'authentic' Créole cuisine. An investigation of the new tourist, or "post-tourist" phenomenon (Poon 1999) venturing off the 'eaten trail' in search of something that is more authentic.

Restaurants, Créole cookbooks, public fairs and festivities, and the expensive dining rooms of foreign-owned luxury hotels where food is served, all present themselves as crucial staging grounds where ideas about Martinique cuisine, and therefore, identity, authenticity and place are continuously tested.

Drinking

As in France, water is safe to drink from the tap, and restaurants will happily serve this at no extra charge (l'eau du robinet).

Fresh fruit juices are also very popular on the island along with jus de canne which is a delicious sugar cane drink which is often sold in vans in lay-bys off the main roads. This juice does not stay fresh for long, so ask for it to be made fresh while you wait and drink it as quickly as possible with some ice cubes and a squeeze of lime.

Martinique is famous for its world class rums and the island today still hosts a large number of distilleries inviting tourist to explore its history. Production methods emphasize use of fresh juice from sugar cane to produce "rhum agricole", rather than molasses widely used elsewhere.

Although rum is far more popular, the local beer in Martinique is Bière Lorraine.

Visas and Vaccinations

Martinique is an overseas department of France so technically it is part of the European Union. This means that the same rules apply to visit Martinique as if traveling to France: US, Canada, Australia, and New Zealand citizens do not need a visa, and will be automatically granted 90 days tourist access upon arrival. Visitors from other EU states do not need a visa either and are free to stay as long as they wish.

Health and Safety

There is no risk of yellow fever in Martinique, although a valid certificate is a requirement to enter. You should get this vaccine six to eight weeks prior to your intended travel date. Although Martinique has high healthcare standards in line with France and the EU, it is recommended you get the following routine vaccinations before you travel: hepatitis A and B, MMR, rabies, tetanus, tuberculosis, and typhoid.

There is absolutely no malaria on the island, so preventative medicine for this is not needed. However, mosquitoes do exist and Dengue fever is prevalent, which cannot be treated, so it is recommended to use bug spray to prevent bites. There is the risk of contracting schistosomiasis if swimming in fresh water areas, which is best avoided, but salt water or chlorinated pools are fine.

Martinique is a very safe country although care should be taken to look after valuables on the beaches. Don't carry large amounts of cash or jewelry. It is best to leave all valuables and your passport in the safe in your hotel. Theft from rental cars is also a small concern so try not to leave your valuables inside in plain sight, even if the vehicle is locked.

Being in the tropics, Martinique is at risk of violent storms and hurricane season lasts from June to November each year, although rarely hit the country directly. Still, it is best to avoid remote areas at this time, and always check weather updates by visiting the US National Hurricane Center website at http://www.nhc.noaa.gov/

Weather

Martinique has a tropical, humid climate with temperatures ranging between 75°F and 85°F year round. The weather is moderated by cool trade winds coming from the northeast, but as you climb in altitude, you can expect about a 10°F drop for every 1,000 ft (the highest peak in the country reaches 4,500 ft).

The rainy season lasts between June and October, seeing up to 9.5 inches in the wettest month of September, compared to only 2.5 in March at the height of the dry season. Martinique still gets tropical storms during the dry season, though, and it will rain for about 13 days a month, although short downpours that shouldn't ruin the day. In September, you can expect nearly double the amount of precipitation, although showers are still sparse during this time.

The hurricane season in Martinique usually runs from June to October, which coincides with the rainy season. The island is rarely hit directly by a tropical cyclone, but you can expect storms passing over the country. Martinique is hit by a devastating cyclone once every eight years on average.

Best Time to Visit Martinique

Most people choose to visit Martinique during the dry season, and the busiest tourist months are between December and April. During this time, accommodation can be booked quickly and prices soar compared to other months. Another spike in prices occurs in July and August, which is Northern Hemisphere's summer, but if you book your travel well in advance you can avoid paying up to twice as much.

July and August are the hottest and most humid months since it is the start of the rainy season, although it does not rain often. By September tropical storms begin to brew, so it is best to avoid being out on a boat at sea. May and June may offer the best deal for visitors as the weather is dry and pleasant, not too humid, and prices are still low. Another good time to visit is right after the rainy season in November when the famous flowers are in bloom.

Seasons

There are two climatic and three tourist seasons on Martinique. The high season is between December and the end of April, with soaring prices and great crowds of travellers. From May to the end of November, Europeans tend to go elsewhere, as the weather is fine back home and travel possibilities are numerous. Summer months (July and August) are a sort of intermediate season, as Martinique and Guadeloupe residents often take advantage of the good weather to visit the mainland. Prices and tourist services, as well as airplane tickets tend to be rather pricy, or even extremely expensive at this period, so be sure to book in advance to avoid paying double.

All in all, if you wish to avoid tourist masses but still take advantage of a pleasant temperature, we would advise you to visit the island in May and June, as the climate in this period of the year is rather dry with an acceptable level of humidity, and tariffs are still quite on the low side. July and August are hot and humid months, but don't be discouraged by tourist clichés saying that the so-called "cyclone" period is a horrible one: it does rain rather often, but the weather is still rather pleasant especially if you are planning to sightsee. Don't count on taking a cruise ship in September, though, as you have considerably higher chances of meeting up with a hurricane or a tropical thunderstorm in this season.

Facts about Martinique and tourism

Martinique, a French Island in the Caribbean area

Martinique Island (with a surface area of 1 100 square kilometres for 400 000 habitants) is one of the richest islands of the region. It distinguishes itself by the presence of a local middle class, a characteristic rarely seen in the region.

As in the case of the other islands of the region, traditional agricultural activities are in full stagnation. Only 7% of the active population works in this sector (dominated by banana, pineapple, sugar cane and rum production). There is a decline in subsidized cultures and the "Sugar Island" is obliged to import sugar beet in order to meet local demand. The industry (less than 15% of the active sectors) is dominated by energy supply enterprises (starting with the oil imported to provide electricity). In these "under-influenced" and dependent economies, characterised by an "over-representation" of civil servants (70% of the actives) and endemic unemployment (30% of the actives) supported by unparalleled social aids in the region and the common practice of undeclared employment, extreme poverty remains scarce (about 500 homeless, mostly foreign people with illegal statuses).

Tourism is the main resource of the island, with revenues in the order of 230 million Euros. This sector officially hires 9% of the active population, dispersed in about one hundred hotels, holiday villages and 200 boarding houses in the country. For a few years now, tourism has undergone a crisis due to the regional competition: a transfer of investments is being carried out to the benefit of the islands which adopt the practice of social dumping (reduced duties, cheap manpower, such as in the Dominican Republic).

The intricacy of human flows in the Martinique Island

As in the case of certain other island territories of the Caribbean basin, this island displays the institutional particularity of a former colony, which has become a French département (since 1946) and belongs today to the European space: it is financially supported by Europe and now receives flows of incoming visitors and new residents coming from the vast zone that is Europe (from

France, Belgium, Germany, Bosnia). The four main categories of mobility are the following:

- ✓ Migrations of autochthonous populations;
- ✓ Tourist flows;
- ✓ Arrival of workers coming from the outside;
- ✓ Passing residents.

The mobility of people from Martinique reveals contradictory movements. During the 1960s to 1980s, the population level remained stable: the balance surplus was compensated by departures encouraged by the French government (jobs reserved in the French administration). From the 1980s, departures are less numerous (local resistance, living in the country) and return flows emerge with emigrants returning to their native island (especially due to changes within the police force, customs and post offices). Incentive policies encourage youngsters to study in France (training assistance, scholarships) but the island now has its own university and students are also attracted to Canada. The French Government is no longer able to control this mobility so easily and the demographic burden on the island is increasing.

The tourists who visit the island are essentially the French (82%), the others being Europeans (9%) and North Americans (7%; above all French-speaking Canadians). The French are highly sensitive to the French-speaking element in a tropical area a fundamental aspect to minimize their impression of being "different". Often, they have never left the French-speaking area during their travels constituting a sort of captive clientele caught between the French Antilles, Quebec and the Maghreb. Among these tourists, one should stress the importance of the natives of Martinique who live abroad, mainly in Paris, who return to their island for the holidays; as indicated by Williams and Hall (2002): "migrants may become tourists in returning to visit friends and relations in their areas of origin".

The foreign workers who settle on the island are of two categories. One must distinguish between migrants coming from areas in difficulty in terms of their economy, and natives of countries where quality of life is superior or equivalent. The first category corresponds to migrants coming from the south. The economic aspects take precedence: these migrants come from neighbouring locations such as the Dominican Islands or Saint-Lucia (GDP/capita inferior to US$ 4,000 per year versus US$ 14,500 in Martinique), namely the very poor countries like Haiti (less than US$ 450 per year and capita). These emigrants work in agriculture, the construction sector and tourism. They constitute the "invisible workers" that nobody talks about as long as the economy is healthy.

The second category corresponds to the French but also European and Canadian emigrants, who come here to reconcile work with quality of life. They often discover the area during their holidays and then decide to try their luck; they sometimes work in tourism notably by developing all the activities which autochthonous populations refuse to carry out for the "whites". Historical disputes have not been settled, and the French authorities give priority to acquiring consensus through subsidies, but forsaking the past which remains a taboo subject. The people in this category, often childless couples (youngsters or young pensioners) in pursuit of well-being allow us to highlight the tourism migration continuum.

The presence of migrants coming from the North is reinforced by new residents, essentially civil servants and other qualified personnel, whose motivations reveal mostly economic opportunities (high salaries, fiscal advantages for pensions), even though these individuals are not insensitive to the environment. Contrary to the emigrants, residents are characterised by an important mobility in their usual practices, not only within the island but also in the region, as well as in relation to their native area. Their presence spans only a few years: there is an important short-term and medium-term turnover with departures to other islands and metropolises. Decisions to leave are determined by difficulties linked to inadequate local education and precarious medical assistance, especially for the elderly.

Circulatory logics are being shaped within the frame of a career project: youngsters gain their professional experience in different tourist locations (between the Indian Ocean, the Western African Coast and the Caribbean Sea) with an evolution in each job (more responsibility).

Officially, the island has 6,500 European and Caribbean emigrants and some 500 clandestines (undoubtedly even more in the squats of the mangrove in Fort-de-France Bay). These figures under-estimate the reality. It is estimated that there are approximately 400 new households established every year on the island.

Sainte Luce: from a fishing village to a tourist resort

The recent evolutions in Sainte Luce (southern sea coast of Martinique) indicate the different transformation phases of this traditional fishing village against the backdrop of the arrival of new residents: a first limited wave in the late 1960s in the old market town, along the sea front, and a second wave in the peripheral residential area since the late 1980s. The increase in land and housing costs trigger a progressive withdrawal of the autochthonous population toward new local authority housing within the territory and further up in the hills. A new spatial organisation is being established between the autochthonous population, migrants, new residents and tourists. Night-time and clandestine connections link the village to the Saint-Lucia Isle, some kilometres further south, through exchanges of stolen car parts, drugs and clandestine passages.

The new territorial organisation in the village of Sainte Luce is similar to that of Martinique Island and the ensemble of Caribbean territories: between the increasingly complex nature of flows, the arrival of new populations ("displaced" local populations, emigrants, tourists, residents) and economic and political issues often covert which require a reflection on the meaning of international and socio-spatial frontiers of the past and present. The territory evolves toward a juxtaposition of enclaves from which the various occupants are unaware of the existence of the other groups of people, each category having its own spatial logic.

From the Martinique Island to the Caribbean Area

A composite and disjointed Area

The contrasts between levels of wealth are just as much frontiers which limit or prohibit human migration in the Caribbean. Tourism, the region's main resource, reinforces economic inequalities. Tourist revenues per capita go from US$ 19,900 in the Cayman Islands (for a population of 35,000 persons), to US$ 8,000 in the Virgin Islands

(121,000 inhabitants), to US$ 4,300 in Antigua and Barbuda, to US$ 2,000 in Saint-Lucia, to US$ 640 in Porto Rico and US$ 7 per capita in Haiti.

In the British Virgin Islands (17,000 inhabitants), tourism produces 45% of the GDP and more than 25% of jobs available. In the American Virgin Islands, two thirds of the jobs are related to tourism. These cramped, barely inhabited island territories attract migrants and clandestines both as destination and transit points. A significant workforce, flexible and with no official status, finds seasonal or longer-term jobs in the tourism sector (catering, hotel-related activities and maintenance activities in general).

Borders preserve tax havens, which are also the most luxurious tourist areas, while other islets are reserved for the richest customers (such as the Nevis Isles or the Mosquito Coast). Other borders tend to contain populations coming from poorer areas like the Dominican Republic, the Central American Coast and of course the stricken island of Haiti. There are also more and more departures from the close Dominican Republic, confronted with an important economic crisis in spite of the good frequentation of these tourist enclaves.

In this context tourist locations constitute privileged places: for a job or a first work experience enabling an individual to adjust to North-American society in the hope of achieving legal migration. The privileged places in this migratory strategy are the American and British Virgin Islands, the Bahamas, Saint Martin. The latter, divided between France and the Netherlands, is not actually separated by any material border. Of the 36,000 inhabitants, the foreign population represents 25%, divided between the people of Haiti (60%) and the

Dominican Republic (20%). Of the 12,000 officially recorded foreigners, 5,000 are clandestine. Since the tourist crisis of the late 1990s "the hunt for clandestines" has been set in motion. Saint Barthélemy, the (tax-free) neighbouring island which receives a top-of-the-range tourism, officially has 6,800 inhabitants and 81 unemployed in 2000. The island needs a foreign workforce, i.e. those "invisible workers". These islands are important transit places for the definitive migrations to the United States.

The mobility theory and the Caribbean

Williams and Balà (2002) invite us to ponder on the "mobility concept starting from a hierachized classification of people's needs". We suggest to split the fourth and last category in two.

The first category corresponds to mobility which responds to a need for survival and individual security, and concerns the refugees and asylum seekers. Departures are made in haste, boat people move during the night and sometimes disappear out at sea (e.g., from Haiti, between extreme poverty and violence, there are mafia gangs such as the "cannibal army").

39The second level is related to the flight from instability and poverty (lack of food and clothes, fulfilment of basic needs). We refer here to the migrants of Haiti, the Dominica, St-Lucia, and all the faceless and nameless people who, with only a few food reserves, go from harbour to harbour of the Caribbean Coast in the hope of being able to sneak into a container ship heading for Miami.

The third level concerns the search for a better economic and social status, the appeal of high salaries. Some migrants are more qualified; we refer here to intra-regional and international movements. They can find an employer who provides them the authorizations to work in foreign countries. But very often, confronted with the lack of legal means to leave their country, they buy forged identity papers (for example of French nationality), then join anglophone islands (St-Lucia, Antigua) while passing themselves off as French West-Indian tourists. And from these places, they buy plane tickets to go to Canada.

The next level corresponds to the temporary movements of consumers on holiday: tourist flows. Tourists are at the origin of financial transfers: they come to consume, not to work

The last level is that of mobility corresponding to the choice of a new living place – namely a new lifestyle: between tourism and daily leisure activities in a more favourable environment and mainly in tourist locations which welcome new residents. We refer here to the whole or partial transfer of a professional activity, in particular in the world of business, entertainment, management of the natural environment and biodiversity. This new mobility remains a prerogative of the well-off classes of rich societies and a handful of the privileged elite from the rest of the world – with a few exceptions. These populations are characterized by a high frequency of movements and by the fact that they have multiple dwellings (the living area is thus divided between several places: between a metropolis of north-southern America and a few privileged tourist locations in the Caribbean. This marginal mobility, which existed since the 19th century in the area with the famous winter residences of businessmen, is more and more developed today. If it remains the prerogative of the most well-off, it now extends to other categories, less fortunate, with a greater variety in the geographical origins and the personal plans.

Ending the Fact

The consolidation of these tourist destinations involves an internationalization of the national economies and an increasing regionalization of the labour market (with unequal implications according to the islands). This economy gives place to greater intra-regional and international mobility.

44The tourist locations of these areas, remote peripheries of North American and European metropolises, constitute channels of entry toward the North for migrants. Very often, these places authorize non-official migrations tacitly because the tourist companies need flexible workers, without qualification, the least heavy possible, to carry out incompressible tasks (gardening, maintenance work). And in the Caribbean basin, the transnational networks with their providers of migrants (from Colombia to Miami) orchestrate an invisible mobility which feeds the illicit activities (in relation to prostitution and drug consumption, grafted in these tourist enclaves), the best example of this being Jamaica.

45Individuals with varied and complex motivations and contrasting movements converge toward tourist locations, which represent mirrors of globalisation. Movements can be made by plane, taxi or bicycle, by migrants, "fake tourists" – and true migrants –, tourists and new residents conveying the image of a world which "runs at several speeds". The analysis of mobility must take social and economic scales into account and one should reflect upon the meaning of new and old frontiers. Similar to crossroads, tourist locations are simultaneously strategic phases – temporary working places and intermediate places – for migrants who wish to reach the rich metropolises of the North. Conversely, they, in turn, also receive populations coming from the North, between holiday stay and new resident status.

46And beyond the Caribbean case, this new mobility, complex, with multiple logics and interferences, can be observed in the Mediterranean islands and coastal areas, on the northern coast of the Philippine Islands or the coastal areas of Australia or New Zeeland. The choice of a living environment and the pursuit of present well-being prevail in the case of these post-migratory movements which characterize the new *living place-workplace-tourist place*continuum).

www.ingramcontent.com/pod-product-compliance
Lightning Source LLC
Chambersburg PA
CBHW021108080526
44587CB00010B/435